Spend Right, Live Right

Practical Spending Tips for Right Living

by C. S. Brown

Spend Right, Live Right
Practical Spending Tips for Right living

Published 2019 by C. S. Brown

All rights reserved.
No part of this publication may be reproduced, stored in a retrieval system, or transmitted by any form or by any means: electronic, mechanical, photocopying, recording, or otherwise, except as may be expressly permitted by the publisher. All requests to reproduce any part of this publication must be submitted in writing and written permission may be granted provided all conditions are satisfied.

The publisher makes no representations or warranties with respect to the accuracy or completeness of the contents of this book and specifically disclaims any implied warranty of merchantability or fitness for a particular purpose. Neither the publisher nor the author shall be liable for any loss of profit or any commercial damages.

Product identity has been protected by the use of pseudo names. Any representation of a product is simply for illustration and no attempt is made to promote or downgrade that product.

Printed in the United States of America

ISBN-13: 978-1986221726
ISBN-10: 1986221725

Dedication

This book is dedicated to those who struggle to make ends meet and wonder if it will ever get any better, for those who need a little help managing their money or resources, and for those who are skillful estate managers, but could manage it better.

[This page intentionally left blank]

Table of Contents

Plan to Spend *9*

Cutting Costs *13*

Increase Your Income *21*

Spend Right *27*

Investments *35*

Financing Major Purchases *51*

Living in the Right Place *53*

Car Buying *57*

Loss Prevention *65*

Live Right *75*

[This page intentionally left blank]

Introduction

My father used to say, "You don't spend money you don't have!" Sounds like practical advice, and while this may be obvious, many of us overlook this fact. If you live in America, you probably do what most people do, "spend now, pay later." And we pay all right - 12%, 18%, 24% and more - in interest! Some of us fall into the "cash advance" mode or "payday loan" and really get into trouble. Then there's the credit cards. So, what leads us down this road of spending money we don't have? How can we reverse this trend?

The purpose of this book is to expose the pitfalls of needless spending and put you on the right path of wise management of your resources. You don't have to be an accountant to follow some simple strategies, nor do you have to be facing bankruptcy to begin. All you need is a desire to have more money in your pocket (or in the bank) and less stress over money to enjoy your life more fully. Even on an average income, you can learn to manage money like a pro and buy that dream house or save for retirement. So, enjoy the journey as you learn how to "spend right, and live right"

C. S. Brown

[This page intentionally left blank]

Chapter 1
Plan to Spend

Develop a Spending Plan

If you are reading this book, then you are probably spending money. *How* to spend your money is the question and spending right requires a plan. You need a plan that includes how much you have to spend and what you will spend it on. Without a plan, you will spend too much, spend it on the wrong things and run out of money before you realize. Decide what you want from life. Do you have a dream of buying a home? A new car? Or would just paying your bills on time be enough? Whatever your aspirations, you need a plan. Start by having a budget.

A budget is a list of all the billing statements from a typical month and the amount of each payment. Include things like rent or mortgage, utilities (electricity, water), auto insurance, car payment, internet and wireless service etc.

Next, make a chart on paper or use a spreadsheet on the computer. List all your expenses in the **left** column and the amount you typically spend in the **right** column. Using a calculator, add the amounts and record it at the bottom of that column. There is an example of this chart on the next page.

If you are using a spreadsheet on the computer, simply plug in the type of expenses in the **left** column and the amount owed in the **right** column. Then plug in your income or total **Take Home Pay** at the top, right. The Table below is based on an average US income for a household of 2 adults. You can adjust the figures based on your income and expenses.

TAKE HOME PAY - Monthly	3500
Rent or Mortgage	1150
Car Payment	350
Auto Insurance	170
Electricity	150
Water Service	120
Same as Cash account	150
Gasoline	160
Food	400
Savings	250
Cable TV Service, Internet, phone	100
Wireless Service	100
Credit Card	100
Charity	200
Medical	100
TOTAL	

When entering the amount of payment for each expense, aim high. Plug in the highest amount you have ever paid in a month, for each expense. The formula bar allows you to "sum" up the values of that column. Just highlight that column, click on **AutoSum** in the menu bar and the **Total** will appear at the bottom. The beauty of a computerized spreadsheet is that it allows you to change values and adjust figures, depending on fluctuations in monthly expenses. For example, in January, the cost of electricity may be much higher due to colder temperatures, but lower in the spring when you aren't using the furnace as much.

Once you complete your **Spending Plan**, look at your list of expenses. Chances are that your total expenses exceed your income! This means you have a debt factor that is accumulating every month. Ouch! I don't need to tell you what this could look like in a year. However, there is a solution, and the purpose of this book is to help you find that solution.

Look again at your list of expenses. What could you live without, at least for a period of time? I found out years ago that I could live without a television. I discovered there were many other things I could do at night and on weekends, besides watch TV. So, seriously ask yourself which expenses can you deduct or reduce on your **Spending Plan**? Now plug in your lowered figures and add up the total amount of expenses. Does it match the amount of your **Take Home Pay**? If not, make a few more adjustments. What about the food you buy? Do you really need to spend that much on food or can you serve soup and salad one day a week? Can you change to a discount food store?

After adjusting your **Spending Plan**, you may discover you need more income, no matter how much you shuffle the figures. In some cases, you might find out you have more money than you thought! I encourage you to play around with the spreadsheet until you make the number at the **top** of the column (your income), match the amount of your expenses at the **bottom** (TOTAL). If you cannot make both ends meet, don't panic. There are a number of things you can do to correct this and make everything work together. The following chapters will cover ways to cut costs, save money and invest money. They are all very doable, even on an average salary.

An add-on to your plan is the "envelope system." This is a method for earmarking certain monies for various expenses. This method works well for cash purchases. The idea is to cash part of your payroll check and divide the money into portions for things like groceries, gas, haircuts, and other miscellaneous expenses. You place the money into individual envelopes and label it. It helps you to allocate cash funds that might otherwise be "lost." It is especially useful for gas money, which is something you don't want to be without. *See last page of book.*

Chapter 2
Cutting Costs

Less is More

The first thing to consider when cutting costs is to use less. Exactly, use less of everything. Now this will take some time, but it can be done. Eat at home, use less ketchup on your burger, one spoonful of peanut butter instead of two. Eat the leftovers instead of feeding it to your pet or throwing it away.

Using less also applies to energy. Take shorter showers, lower the thermostat, and hand wash the dishes. This uses less water. Always wash a full load of laundry and use the "cold" setting. This saves on electricity and reduces the electric bill. Use less gasoline, by planning your trips to the store, so you are not going in 5 different directions.

Use less paper goods. Use one napkin at the dinner table (I buy the good ones and one is enough). Use dish towels for drying surfaces, instead of paper towels. What about those plastic grocery bags? Why buy trash can liners for the bathroom when you can use those?

Once you develop a mindset of using less of everything, you will think of other ways to use less food, less water, and less energy. Ultimately, this will help you to spend less money and cuts your costs. Then you will have more money for other things or finally catch up on your bills. Less is definitely more.

Buy the dinner, drink the water

My husband and I enjoy going out on weekends, exploring a nearby city or a walk along a waterfront. This is a very inexpensive way to enjoy time together. Afterwards, we usually have dinner at a restaurant or just settle for a basket of fries. In previous years, we just randomly went out, spent too much money and then later regretted it. We told ourselves that we deserved it, whether we had the money or not. There was no planning involved. Then we always bought the drinks and had the refills along with our meal. Sometimes the beverages cost as much as one entrée.

Eventually, we learned that we needed a plan for our outings. So, we used the envelope system for this. Every payday I put about $40 in an envelope and marked it: *Weekend*. That set a limit on spending. Now we pay closer attention to the menu and just get the water! You can also request a menu before you are seated and check the prices and the entrees. (Do I really want to eat here?). Then you can decide if this is where you need to be. We are not opposed to walking right out the door and finding another place to eat if the food is not pleasing or the prices are beyond our budget.

Going out a lot, though, can hurt your budget. This is also a time that a credit card can really get you into really big trouble. So, plan your outings, make sure you can afford to go out and yes, order the water! "Water, please, with lemon!"

Speaking of water, I want to show you how much you can save by ordering the water at a restaurant, instead of purchasing expensive drinks and refills. Here's a little math calculation to show you what I mean.

If a couple goes to a restaurant or buys fast food, 8 times a month and purchases two sodas each time, at an average cost of $2.50 per drink, that would be $40.00 a month. Over a year's time that would add up to be about $480.00 and over 20 years it would be about $9,600. Now add to that amount, 2 kids. The amount would double to $19,200 or approximately $20,000! Then think about all the other times you stop at a convenience store to buy beverages or a cup of coffee on the way to work. How about those hot summer days that you stop to get cold drinks? Have you ever wondered how much money you were spending on beverages?

I would estimate that most families spend a lot more on beverages and snacks than they realize. It's just something that many people are accustomed to doing. They have not stopped to think about how much they are spending. The $20,000 I mentioned could be invested into a retirement account and by the time you retire, it could double in value depending on your age when you start and the rate of return. Why would you miss that opportunity?

The point is, drinking water can save you a lot of money and you will be healthier too. You can do the same thing at home. Avoid purchasing so many sodas, juices or other sugary drinks. Drink water!

Bring Your Own Snack

Whenever I stop to gas up my car at a full-service gas station, I am always amazed at the amount of snack food that people buy. Here I am standing in line to pay for my fuel and the young man just ahead of me is holding 2 cans of *Rip Roar*, 1 candy bar and 1 large pretzel. The clerk rings up the sale for a total of $8.72.

Next in line, is a middle-aged woman with a *Mountain High*, a large cinnamon roll, and a packaged brownie. Cost: $6.38.

Then it's my turn and I give the clerk a $30.00 to pay for a fill-up. I have to admit that the cinnamon roll looks good, but I have to remind myself that I am only there to buy gas!

If you read the statistics concerning the amount of snack food that Americans purchase every year, you would be astounded. Some people eat more snacks than *real* food.

We all know that snack food is not particularly healthy and it is expensive. We won't even mention the amount of trash or litter generated by this popular habit. Yet, we continue to buy it, consume it and reap the rewards of excess weight gain and a drained wallet. I have observed people spend their last $10.00 on snack food, rather than put gas in their car and then ride to work on empty!

Carry a case of water in your car and keep snacks with you. I usually have some kind of snack food in my car or purse for emergencies! It comes in handy when you just get off of work.

Another time you might be prone to stopping for snack food or drinks, is when shopping for the day or taking a day trip. When you know you are going to be gone from the house for an extended period of time, fill a small cooler with cold drinks and sandwiches and fruit. Bring granola bars or similar which are easy, because they require no refrigeration. They are good to keep in your car as well and they only take a minute to grab on your way out the door.

Planning ahead in this way will keep you from spending money on fast food, snacks and drinks and you can tell yourself, "I'm saving money, keeping myself hydrated and enjoying a nutritious snack."

What's in Your Wallet?

A nice little add-on in your wallet is a gift card. They can be used for all kinds of things. It also limits spending. Let's say for example, you have a tendency to stop at 6/12 for coffee in the morning. No one's perfect! You can purchase a gift card that can be reloaded and used for that. Add $10 bi-weekly or $20 for the month. This allows you to stop maybe once or twice a week for coffee. Bring your own thermos and save even more with a refill. With the money you save, buy your own coffee pot later and make it at home. It's a lot cheaper. You could even give up coffee and switch to water!

A lot of cash in your wallet is probably not a good idea for some people. It may be too easy to spend. Debit and credit cards carry the same threat for others. So, what do you do?

Decide what works best for you to limit spending. Personally, I don't carry a lot of cash and I rarely carry a debit card. I prefer the gift cards (reloadable) and the envelope system for cash. I only take out what I will be spending that day. I do carry a credit card for emergencies, but I will admit, it's tempting to use it for the wrong thing.

Some statistics show that many Americans have an average of $25,000 in credit card debt. I share this as a word of caution when charging anything. Always ask yourself if it's part of the plan and do you really need it? If you must use a card for purchases, when you do get your statement in the mail, pay it within the billing period in full. This way you don't have to pay interest. This means you have to limit the amount you charge; a debt you can afford to pay back, on time.

So, what do you do when your credit card debt is over the top? The first thing you can do is cut the cards up! STOP using the cards. Then you need a plan to pay them off. If it's a large amount, you can secure credit counseling to help you develop a plan. They might be able to consolidate your debts and get the total amount reduced. Once you have a figure, you will need to make a monthly payment to pay off the debt. Then go back to your original **Spending Plan** and make the adjustments. If you find that you cannot fit the new expense into your plan, then eliminate something else – maybe discontinue your TV, internet or home phone service. If that does not cover the cost, then you may need to get a 2nd job. This is discussed in detail in the next chapter. Whatever you do, avoid claiming bankruptcy if it's at all possible. A bankruptcy can affect your credit score and it can take years to improve it.

There was a time when I owed close to $21,000 in credit card debt and loans. To be honest, it was overwhelming. So, I sat down and looked over everything with a calculator and discovered that it was indeed possible to pay this off! That alone, made me feel better. So, I made a plan and cut all my expenses to the extreme. I even lost weight (that's a good thing) during those few years because I wasn't buying snack foods or anything extra. I did not go to the movies or restaurants and I did not have cable, internet or a home phone. There were many other things I did without to cut expenses. I even had to move to a less expensive place. I left a luxury apartment and moved into a one bedroom flat in a low-income area. (I was single at the time). There was no gym on site, no tennis courts and no walking trails! In addition, I got that 2nd job and little by little I tackled that debt. It took me 3 years to do it, but I got through it and I learned that all I needed was a plan. I also learned that using a credit card can be very costly and that I needed to heed my father's advice, by not spending more than I had.

I don't always get it right and some of that I will share in this book. But I will say, that having a **Spending Plan** is the best thing I've ever done to keep me on track or to get me back on track when I deviate. Also know that whatever kind of mess you have gotten yourself into with money, can be resolved. It may not be obvious at first, but there is always something you can do to make things better. My hope is that I have provided some tools in these chapters to help you manage your money, cut your expenses and make you way out of debt.

Chapter 3

Increase Your Income

Moonlighting

If you have discovered that a 2nd job is what is needed, then by all means pursue it. There are many options for finding a second job, depending on your line of work. Waiting tables on weekends has been a favorite for many who need supplemental income. Retail stores offer many part time positions for a few nights a week, as well. Amusement parks, tourist attractions and call centers, especially in the summer, could be just the ticket to earn extra income. Babysitting, cleaning homes or offices, or even a cottage industry. You can also ask coworkers, family members and friends who just may have some connections. And when all else fails, there is the internet you can surf. There are many websites dedicated to this kind of thing.

When taking on a second job, it may require you to make some sacrifices and many other adjustments. You might not have time to watch TV, go to the gym or play pool with the guys. You may feel more tired than usual. However, it is usually well worth it for most people who want to pay off debt or build their savings account. And it may prove be a very good experience. You might make some new friends or discover some things about yourself you never knew. It might even lead to a new career!

Sell it, List it, Pawn it!

Everyone has stuff that they don't need. Yes, I know, it was a good idea at the time and it promised so much. I remember the time I bought a food dehydrator. I paid plenty for that and used it once. No one said it would take all night to dry sliced apples! Or how about the year I bought a 9 x 11-foot trailer for my tiny economy car to pull. Of course, the car did not have a hitch so I paid for that to be installed as well. How many times do you think I used that? And since I didn't have a decent driveway to store it (always consider those kinds of things) it was dragged into the backyard behind the tool shed. It collected lots of leaves and stray cats, who found it a great place to lie in the sun. When we wanted to use it, we couldn't back the car up to hitch it up, so we had to pull it by hand (no small feat) to the front driveway to connect it to the car. Whew! We got tired of that and finally sold it to a home builder who made better use of it. So, what do you have that you can sell?

A good place to look is in the attic, garage (if you have one), tool shed, back yard (Do you really use that grill?) or in closets. So, what do you have that you can live without?

A yard sale is a good way to sell stuff you don't really need. Someone will think what you have to sell is wonderful! Now if you have never had a yard sale, it's really quite easy.

Just figure out when it's a good time by checking the weather and availability of helpers. Then find a location to have it. If you own a home, your backyard is a perfect location. If you live in an apartment, you might be able to team up with a friend who owns a home. Some cities have flea markets with booths that you can rent for a small fee.

Once you decide on a location, you may need to get a permit. They are generally not very expensive. Check with your local city hall about obtaining a permit.

Concerning a sign, you really only need one at the front of your property or booth. (There are laws about where you can post a yard sale sign, so be aware of that. You cannot nail a sign to a telephone pole!)

Next, place an ad in the newspaper (they will help you over the phone) and just have your tables set up by 7 AM the day of the sale. Most avid yard sale shoppers read the newspaper and look for yard sales and they're looking for a bargain. Be willing to negotiate the price. Anything you sell is a profit, especially if it's just been sitting in your garage collecting dust.

When you open your sale for business, always have a

"bank" of about $50.00 to start and include coins. Wear one of those nail pouches that you can purchase at your local hardware store for very little money. Keep all your money on you! I remember the year I had a yard sale and the cash box was just sitting on the table. It walked off and it left me in shock. So, watch your money and watch your stuff. If you have to leave for a moment to take care of something, make sure you let someone take over. It's never a good idea to leave the area unattended. You might miss a sale, too.

If having a yard sale is an impossibility for you, then you might consider selling your stuff online. Expensive items that you think you can sell for a much higher price, can be listed under classifieds on many popular websites – designed for this purpose. If you are not familiar with these, surf the web using the key word, "classified." Things like furniture, appliances or electronics would bring in a better profit when sold on these kinds of websites. I knew of a situation with a family member who was moving. He had a large dining room set that simply would not fit in his new place, so he listed it under the classifieds on a reputable website. It sold right away.

Another way to sell things you don't really need is a consignment shop. Some of us have a reserve of serviceable clothing in our closet that we will never wear. What about that expensive gown you bought and used only once? What about the tuxedo, suits, coats and/or career clothing? There are some shops that sell children's clothing, exclusively. We all know that children outgrow many of their clothes before they wear out. These items can be sold and the commission can be used for replacements.

Furniture can also be taken to consignment shops for sale. Oversized sofas or desks would be excellent items to sell, but keep in mind that the commission you would make may take a while to receive. Consignment stores should be considered residual income. I would attempt to sell your costly items online, first. You will most likely get the highest price and it tends to sell quicker.

Pawn shops can be very helpful also, when you need cash in a hurry! (I would avoid any kind of "cash advance" place that require you to pay interest or "payday loans.") Pawn shops will generally accept tools, electronics, CD's, DVD's, bicycles and jewelry (silver or gold). Tools, and electronics taken to a pawn shop must be in working order. If you pawn a cell phone or a tablet, be sure to have the charger with it and charge it up, first. CD's and DVD's should be in the original case. Bicycles should be in working order and look clean. Gold or silver jewelry can be broken, because the pawn shops will sell it to another dealer, based on ounces. Gold brings in the highest price. You can also pawn musical instruments such as keyboards, drums, and brass horns, etc. A pawn shop may not give you a lot, but if you are in a spot, this might be exactly what you need. They will give you cash money and you are out the door.

Have I ever frequented a pawn shop? Absolutely! I have pawned a number of things in my day. One day my gas tank in my car was on empty and it was a few days before payday. I took all my movies and sold them. It was just enough money to fill my gas tank and buy a few other things. (How many times are we going to watch the same movies, anyway?) A TV brings in a good price, too!

If you do decide to pawn a few tools or give up your TV, they will ask for your ID. Don't feel intimidated by this requirement. They are required by local or state laws to ask for your identification. Whatever shop you go to, it would be a good idea to call, first, and ask if they are accepting the merchandise you have for "sale." Sometimes, they have an abundance of a particular good but they may be "buying" a product you haven't thought of selling.

Chapter 4

Spend Right

Get the Free Phone

I have stood in the phone section at a well know wireless company to purchase a phone, several times. And yes, the prices can be astronomical and many people buy them anyway! I was one of those people once upon a time, but I have since learned that there is another way to buy a phone. Get the free one or almost free! While there is an activation fee, it is still a serious savings to you and you are not without a phone. You must be careful, though, because the case for it could cost more than the activation fee. To resolve this, go online and purchase a case later or search a discount store for one. It is suggested that you don't wait too long to do this. Dropping a cell phone is more common that you think and you don't want to do that without a hard case to protect the phone.

The free cell phones that are offered at a wireless retail store may be contingent upon signing up for service for a period of time. If you are on a tight budget, this might be for you.

You can also purchase cell phones online that are older models for a lot less than the latest and greatest! For example: The *QRX-S6* sells for $800, but you can buy the *QRX-S2* for a lot less and it is exactly what you need. Try to avoid going on an ego trip over a phone. In the big picture, a balanced budget is better than showing off your new phone.

I do remember when I had a flip phone, which by the way, was the coolest when it first came out. Then there was the *Blueberry*. I felt so insecure because I still had a flip phone and my coworkers were all using a *Blueberry*! And then there was the *Superphone!* I was perhaps the last person on earth to get one. But I got it free! Yes, really. It was an older model but worked just fine, once I figured out how to use it. (I admit I went to that class that shows you how to work it). So, please don't stress if you still have a flip phone or some other older model. Remember the purpose of a phone – to communicate.

A real concern about people who own a *Superphone* is the amount of time they spend texting, surfing or talking and forget there are real people around them. Just watch people in a public place and see how many have their eyes glued to their phones and miss so much of what is going on around them. It's the children that tend to be ignored and the couples who are not attentive to one another. I suppose I could write a whole book about the unintended consequences of cell phones, but I won't.

When looking for a cell phone online, make sure the phone is compatible with your provider service. You know which one! You can also get your cell phone case online at the same time. Sometimes there are discount codes you can enter for additional savings. Also, look for the free shipping.

Another expense concerning cell phones is the cost of insurance that they want you to buy. It might not really save you much, especially if your phone was free. You pay $15 a month for a year to insure it ($180 yearly), and then drop it in the toilet! Just pocket the $180 and go get another inexpensive phone. Remember, you are trying to cut expenses. If you get a flip phone or some other version, you don't need the insurance or a data package, and that saves you money.

Again, don't worry about keeping up with other people who have the latest and the greatest cell phone. They may be paying $500 - $900 for that phone! They might also have a high credit card debt. Stick with your **Spending Plan** no matter what. It's more important to maintain a budget than to enjoy a fleeting moment of bliss!

Smart Shopper

The trend today is to have a membership at a Wholesale club. An old friend of mine called it the $100 store because she never left without spending at least that much. Nowadays, I doubt you can get out the door, at that rate. Do you really need that? Does it really save you money or are you spending more money than you have? I would guess the latter is true. So where do you shop to save money on food and clothing?

There are a number of discount grocery stores and clothing stores in every city. Find them and go there. If some of the "off brands" make you uncomfortable, then research the manufacturer. Read the reviews of the product. It may help you decide what to buy. I keep my *Superphone* handy when shopping for clothing, food or small appliances. I look up the product, if I'm concerned about a purchase. Sometimes it's just a name brand you are not familiar with, but it's popular in another city or state. Sometimes it's a division of a larger company. If I'm still not sure, I read the label or specs carefully. You can always just buy a few things at a discount store and the rest at a "trustworthy" retailer. If there is a problem with the product after you purchase it, keep your receipts and return it.

When you do shop at the mall or the "anchor stores" shop the sales and the clearance racks, first. It may take some time, but if you are patient, you will find the gold. Avoid paying full price when you can get it for less.

Another thing to consider when buying clothing is to ask yourself, "Do I want to spend 2 hours in a dressing room or can I just take it home and try it on there?" Unless you are shopping out of town, take it home. Trying on clothes in a store can really wear you out. And being tired while shopping, tends to lead to bad decisions about purchases. Besides, those small dressing rooms are not very flattering and you can't really get an idea of the fit sometimes. And as always, keep your receipts.

When buying groceries, the biggest mistake shoppers make is purchasing too many processed foods. They may seem convenient, but already prepared foods are more expensive than home cooking and not as healthy. Processed foods can take a toll on your body over the long run, causing high cholesterol, diabetes and a number of other maladies. Processed foods are high in salt, saturated fats, sugars and chemicals that you can't even pronounce. Did you ever wonder what cellulose is? It's a common ingredient in ice cream and grated or powdered cheese, like *Romano*. Cellulose is found in a plant such as cotton and it is often used to make paper, plastic and fabrics! Do you really want this in your body?

So, buy the chunk cheese and grate it yourself. In fact, buy all-natural products as much as possible and cook the meals yourself. It may not be convenient right now, but it will save you money in the long run and help you keep a healthy body. A sickly body can be very expensive to maintain.

Thrift Stores

Along with food, we buy kitchen items and furniture. These tend to be expensive purchases. How do you cover the cost of these things? Believe it or not, you can find kitchenware and furniture in thrift stores. In fact, you can find a lot of things at a thrift store! Here are a few unknown facts about them.

Thrift stores offer new or "like new" items. These items are sold or donated by large retailers. They also come from "damaged" shipments and the salvaged items are sold in thrift stores. Other times they are "overruns" or cancelled orders. Whatever the reason, you can find quality goods at a thrift store and it will ultimately save you money.

Look for kitchen tools, glassware, pots, pans and flatware. You might even find a replacement for a set of glasses or a lid for your favorite pot. Just wash and sterilized everything in the dishwasher before using in your home. Say what? Have you ever eaten at a restaurant? You do realize that all of the pots and pans, dishes and flatware are used, washed, and used again!

Most thrift stores have plenty of furniture. It can be cleaned, painted or refinished (if you are handy) and look great in your apartment or house. There is a new kind of paint you can get at the paint store for repainting furniture. You only need to wash the wood down and maybe lightly hand sand it. The paint adheres without additional primer and it looks great. You can even add distressed marks to give it a vintage look. I have seen these kinds of pieces at gift shops and furniture stores for a very high price. So, don't be afraid to go treasure hunting at your nearest thrift store. I always say, "Who's going to know?"

Shopping Online

Online buying can save you money and time. Personally, I order a lot of things online, with amazing savings. Some retailers sell the same merchandise they carry in the story, online at a reduced price. Many of the large retailers (you know who they are) also offer sales and clearance items. You can buy clothes, shoes, window treatments, books, pet food and water filters to name a few. Some orders qualify for free shipping. Select the lowest rate if you have to pay for shipping. That will save you money. I have even ordered pet flea meds for my cat at a considerable discount.

A word of caution about online buying: know who you are dealing with. If you are unfamiliar with internet shopping, stick with the reputable businesses, which generally have retail stores as well. And if you don't like the product, you can return it at the store. When I need an item, I have not been able to find in a retail store or at familiar sites, I read the reviews. I have taken a few chances and received the merchandise in new condition with no problems.

Additionally, always save the packing slips and packaging for online orders for a couple of weeks, to be sure you are satisfied with the product. It's a lot easier to return the item if you have the original packaging and proof of purchase. Over time, you will become savvier with online shopping.

[This page intentionally left blank]

Chapter 5

Investments

Savings Accounts

Many adults will work up to 50 years or more in their lifetime. Their income will tend to ebb and flow over those years. There may be times of plenty, lean times, and everything in between. Whatever your income, saving a portion of it is wise. Saving money every month should be a part of your **Spending Plan.** I call saving money, "delayed spending," because eventually you will spend that money. There are many ways to save money.

Begin by saving a reasonable amount every month, given your level of income. Examine your **Spending Plan** and decide what you can save and still pay your expenses. Once you figure that out, enter it into your **Spending Plan**.

You can also add additional savings from overtime pay or a bonus. Resist the temptation to "celebrate" the windfall by going to dinner or the movies. Being spontaneous has its place, but it can sabotage your budget. Make your dinner and movie dates a part of your **Spending Plan.** Do the same with your income tax refund – save it. Aim to save the amount of money you would need for one month's expenses over the year. Based on the budget on P. 10, that would be $3500 a year in savings.

Regular Savings

Savings should be short-term and long-term. A regular savings account can be considered short-term. The purpose of a regular savings account is to cover those unexpected expenses that are not a part of your **Spending Plan**. These expenses include things like car repairs or maintenance, that suit or dress you need to attend a wedding or special event, or to replace a small appliance. You can also pull out money from this account for a bill that is higher than usual like a medical bill or a utility bill. Some people call this a "slush fund."

While your goal is to save a month's salary during the year, you may have to catch up on bills before you can begin to do that. Start where you can: $25.00 or $50.00 a month and increase this amount when possible. The easiest way to save in a regular savings account is to set up an automatic draft on your checking account. This is a good worry-free method.

You can also set up short-term savings for things like holiday shopping or vacations. Some employers offer this option. Decide what amount you think you will need and divide by 12. Deposit that amount in that account every month. When the event occurs, you won't have to wonder how you will cover the cost. It's already set aside for you. A modest amount might start at $300-$500 a year. Obviously, this kind of account would only be possible if your income allows it.

Retirement Accounts

Long-term savings come in the form of Retirement Plans such as 401K, IRA, ROTH – with interest rates that far exceed a regular savings account. These accounts can provide a tax shelter for your income called a "pre-tax contribution." The money is taken directly out of your payroll check and invested for you. If you get this through your employer, it's a good plan. I have participated in a retirement plan through my employment for many years, and the return is well worth it. It may seem like your check is a little short when you first start, but after a few years you will see it differently. And, when you turn 59 ½ you can make withdrawals to cover things like large hospital bills or emergencies (property damage, appliance failures, death in the family, etc.).

Most employers who offer these plans, will bring in representatives, who will meet with you to discuss the various retirement plans. This is one thing you don't want to bypass. Too many people fail to plan for retirement or if they do, it's very late in life. If you don't think you can spare a lot for this kind of investment, then start small, but start! The interest on your money will grow at a greater rate than a regular savings account. If you begin depositing money in a retirement account around the age of 30, by the time you reach 65, you will have a nice little nest egg. According to statistics, many people do not save for retirement or put it off. So, be smart, start asap.

Home Investment

Are you wondering why I included home buying under investments? This is because a home is what you will spend most of your money on over a lifetime. I am an advocate for home ownership, because it is an investment that typically appreciates over time. The benefits outweigh the challenges for most home owners. This is why I believe everyone, who is able, should buy a home. The fact that most of your income will be invested in some kind of housing, why not own the property that you have been paying for every month?

I am by no means, an expert on home buying. There are many books on the market that address this topic in detail, and I do recommend you buy or borrow one before making a purchase. I will offer a few tips that may get you to think about buying a home or at least get you started.

Owning a home can often be less expensive than renting an apartment. This is because you will have your home paid off at some point, while rent is for a lifetime. Having your own home paid for when you reach your senior years, can make all the difference. Too many elderly people who don't own a home, are forced to live in low-income housing. Living on social security, combined with the rising costs of rent, a luxury apartment is not an option. That's the advantage of owning a home. A home mortgage tends to be a fixed rate, so eventually you get ahead of the rent and at some point, there is no monthly payment at all! This will be appreciated on a fixed income.

For example, suppose you buy a home for $200,000 and your loan is financed for 30 years. Your monthly payment, depending on the interest rate, could be around $1150. In 30 years, the cost for an apartment (less square footage, no doubt) could be double that amount. You might even notice a difference in what you pay for your home, in the first five years. compared to the rising cost of rent. Your mortgage is still $1150 but the rent you would be paying is $1500 a month for the same or less square footage.

A home also offers you more privacy and a sense of your own space. For example, nothing beats having your own backyard when you have friends or family over for a barbeque. If you have kids, they have plenty of space to play. You can let the dog loose to run around the yard, when you just don't feel like taking that long walk.

There is also more storage space in a home. Most homes have an attic, garage and/or tool shed. No more monthly checks written for storage facilities. Overall, you just have more room and more windows!

I remember the time I lived in that 1-bedroom apartment and there were only 2 windows and 1 sliding glass door. When I bought a home after that, I walked through the place counting the windows. There were 13 windows, total. It was amazing!

There are many other benefits to owning a home. As I mentioned earlier, pick up one of those books that explores, in-depth, the value of owning your own home.

Dream Home

Once you decide that home ownership is for you, then you need to plan for it. You will need to have access to some money during the pre-qualifying process. Think: $10,000 at the very least, if you are a first-time home buyer. When you buy a house, you typically need 5-20% of the selling price as a down-payment. Then you will need money for the closing cost which varies depending on a lot of things. For example, if the home you are interested in buying, sells for $150,000, then 5% of that value is $7500, which you will need for a down payment. The closing cost is added to this amount, but often the seller will pay all or some of this cost, which can really help! With some loans, there are exceptions to the "down payment" rule. You may have no down payment or a small amount to pay.

You will also need money for an appraisal of the property and a home inspection. These fees are usually out-of-pocket expenses. Your realtor can give you those exact figures.

There are other expenses, too, once you move in, like window treatments, rugs, locks, and possibly furniture when you move in. If you have moved at least once, then you know that the curtains you had in your old place, just won't do in the new place.

The first thing I always do when I move, is buy blinds for all the windows (unless I am blessed with some already installed). Nothing looks worse than sheets hanging over the windows! And you can get the $5.00 ones to start with.

Saving for a Home

There are many creative ways to save for a home. I knew of a family who rented a trailer (inexpensive) for 8 years and with the money they saved, bought a new home. Some newlyweds live with their parents for a few years and save up for a down payment on a home. You can also rent a very inexpensive apartment and save until you have reached your goal. As long as you remember that those situations are temporary and for a higher purpose, you can do it.

While you are saving to buy a home, do your research. There are many websites that show homes for sale. You can go to the main sites for home sales and learn a lot from searching. Find out everything you can about what to look for including the neighborhoods. Also consider what you can reasonably afford.

Home Loans

Before you go looking for a home, you will need to discuss with your bank, what kind of loan you qualify for and go through a pre-approval process to find out how much house you can afford. The bank will look at your debt to income ratio and your credit score. This is why it is important to protect your credit by paying your bills on time. (Your credit score says a lot.) They will also ask for proof of income and a range of other things that your bank will tell you about. The pre-approval process is usually done quickly. It is often recommended that you go to at least two lending institutions. I always use my own bank and check with one other lender.

Your income to debt ratio is based on your total income and the amount you owe on credit. The ratio is calculated as a percentage. The debt the bank looks at includes credit cards, car loans, and any other credit accounts. Getting these accounts paid off or lowering the balance will help you tremendously when applying for a home loan.

Your credit score is a huge factor when buying anything

on credit, especially a home. A 750-850 is considered "excellent," 700-749 is "good," and 650 or below is "fair to poor." If you find that your credit score limits you too much, ask those courageous questions about how to improve your score. Then reapply in a year or two for a home loan.

Once you get your pre-approval for a home loan, check your **Spending Plan**. If the bank affords you $1400 a month, that may technically be too much. Challenge yourself to find a home with a lower monthly payment than the bank is willing to lend you, or one that comfortably fits your budget. You will need money for yard tools, landscaping, repairs and replacements that you cannot foresee at this time. Too many home buyers get too much house and live to regret it later. Just look at the foreclosure market!

House Hunting

A single-family home is what most people buy, with at least 3 bedrooms. If you ever move, a 3-bedroom home sells a lot better than a 2 bedroom. I would only buy a 2-bedroom if you plan to stay there. Another important thing to look for is the number of bathrooms. Having one bathroom can be a real challenge! When you find a home you really like, then there are some vital questions to ask before proceeding any further. Try not to get overly excited and forget to ask about the following:

1. Age of the house – if the home is over 30 years old then you need to know if any upgrades have been made to plumbing, electrical, etc.

2. Age of the roof, HVAC (heating, ventilation, air-conditioning) water heater, and appliances

3. Type of plumbing: PVC, copper, PEX, CPVC

4. All Electric, Natural Gas, or both

5. Large trees on the property

The condition of the home is very important, because having to replace any of the aforementioned is very costly. As a general rule, any appliance older than 10 years will need to be replaced soon. A roof or a furnace may last 20 years. Tree removal can be very expensive and their roots can interfere with the plumbing inside and outside of the home. When you negotiate on the price of the home (making an offer) you can ask for the upgrades before making your purchase or you can offer a lower price to cover the cost of these upgrades. You can also ask for tree removal as part of the contract. Check with your realtor and work something out. Be bold!

Before you settle on a home, give it plenty of thought. You may experience a lot of pressure to buy now. Remember, it's your money and it's your life. That is not the only house on the market. Ask your realtor to show you a few more homes. It may help you decide what you want. You might want to wait awhile or consider buying a *Fixer Upper*!

Fixer Uppers

If you are handy and don't have a lot of money to work with, a *Fixer Upper* just might be for you. There are contractors out there that can do the repairs on a "pay as you go" basis. If you can do most of the work yourself, that's even better. If you do buy a *Fixer Upper*, make sure the price is very reasonable. Otherwise, it could cost more than a new home.

When making repairs or upgrades, be prepared to be inconvenienced a lot, while the house is under construction. It can be very messy, too, and you will have to do a lot of cleaning. You will need to cover your furniture and many other items, as the dust that accumulates will be over the top. And speaking of "time" it will take a lot of time to finalize some projects. You may need to get city permits and inspections. This is protocol for certain upgrades such as electrical, plumbing and even adding a new deck. This is for your protection, but it can take a minute for the inspector to come out. The positive side is that you could save a lot of money and end up with a very nice custom home. And for those who love a challenge, this might be just what you need.

Home Warranty

When negotiating about the home, get the home warranty and ask for the seller to pay for it. This is usually how things work, but don't assume anything. Just ask. A home warranty can be a real plus to help cover the cost of replacing a water heater, repairing the HVAC system, and all your kitchen appliances, etc. It can save you a lot of money if you get the right kind of warranty. Again, do your research and find out which company offers the best home warranty and read the reviews. You can also talk to friends or coworkers and find out this information. If you do get the home warranty, it is usually good for 1 year. You will need to renew it the 2nd year and pay the policy. They are not that expensive.

Selling Your Home

So, you've lived in your home now for 7 years and it's time for a bigger place. You are about to embark on another journey: Selling your current home. Find a realtor who believes in the value of your home and is enthusiastic about selling it. Your realtor will give you advice on how to get the most return on your home. After all, you want to make money on the sale of your home, not lose money. Some of the things your realtor might suggests to make your home more marketable:

- Fresh coat of paint on the house
- Landscaping and manicured lawn
- Working appliances and a dishwasher
- HVAC, water heater, electrical and plumbing all in working order
- Flooring, windows and doors in good condition

What you can sell the home for depends largely on the market and the area in which you live. You might have paid too much for your home and then discover that homes in your area are not bringing in what you expect. This is where you need to be flexible about the asking price. Your realtor will guide you in this area when you decide on a selling price. This is where the emotions tend to get in the way. You have most likely become attached to your home and see all the wonderful things about it so, you don't want to just give it away. You are also aware of all the maintenance you did to the property. Because of these factors, your assessment of the property is probably not aligned with what you could sell it for. Hang in there!

If you are one of the "lucky ones" and your home has miraculously doubled in value, you might be in a position to lower the price for the new buyer, who may happen to be a first-time home owner. There is always an element of charity in us.

Once your home is listed for sale, you will be expected to keep the home neat and tidy. They also want you to be flexible about the times they can show the home. This can be challenging. Your realtor will show the home to prospective buyers, but they prefer that the owners are not home. So, be prepared to pack it up on a moment's notice to head out to the mall or the neighborhood park.

When you do sell your home, the profit you make will cover the cost of the realtor (who gets a commission from the sale of the home) and your down payment on your next house. Resist the temptation to spend this money on other things. Put it right back into your next home, which may cost you more, anyway.

Selling Tips

I have owned several homes and "when to sell" is very

important. The spring and summer seasons tend to bring people out, looking at homes. If you can wait until this time, do so.

If someone is interested in your home, the realtor will share their notes about customer "requests" and comments. Pay close attention to this, but don't make any repairs or changes until the buyer actually makes an offer and the upgrades are in writing. Try to make up for the cost of upgrades with the selling price. For example, if the home is selling for $200,000 and the customer wants a new roof, don't come down on the asking price too much. That could be $10,000+ out of pocket for you.

Check for "curb appeal." When someone drives past your home, what do they see? Flowers planted in the front beds can be just the ticket or patio furniture (buy bright colors – the plastic ones at a discount). And by all means, keep the grass mowed and edged. Paint the front door and wash the windows!

Home Inspections

When you buy a home or sell yours, there will be a home inspection of each property. Sometimes the findings are enormous. Don't panic. If you are buying, you can request that these repairs be done by the seller at their cost. They may agree to all of them, some of them or none of them. If they don't plan to make the repairs, you can negotiate the price of the home. Work with your realtor to learn what is reasonable. If you are selling your home. You have the option of doing all, some or none of the repairs as well.

Keep in mind that when you are buying a home, the inspector may miss some things or major on the minors. After all, they are serving the seller. You can do your own inspection and look the house over thoroughly. All that's "wrong" with a house may not actually be discovered though, until you live in that home. Trust me, I know! That's why the home warranty should be purchased when you buy that house. The seller typically pays for that and you should insist that they do.

Chapter 6

Financing Major Purchases

Same as Cash Accounts

So, you bought your first home, or maybe you've been in your home for years and the dryer went out or the furnace needs replacement. If you bought the home warranty, it may be a simple fix and you will only have to pull a few hundred out of your savings. For those of you who don't have the warranty, or enough in your savings account, you will need to find another way to pay for a new dryer or furnace.

There are several home improvement businesses who offer "same as cash" accounts. Depending on the total amount financed, you could qualify for 6 months or up to 24 months. You simply make a monthly payment. There is no interest charged if you pay off the account within the specified time. The best way to determine your monthly payment is to take your total purchase amount and divide by the number of months you have to pay it off. If you only pay the minimum required amount, which is typically $25.00, you will end up paying interest.

For example, if the dryer costs $700, and they give you 6 months to pay for it, then you would need to make 6 payments of $117 approximately. The account would be paid in full at the end of the 6 months and you would pay NO interest.

Same as Cash accounts are generally offered at home improvement stores for large appliances, HVAC, water heaters, fencing, roofing and many other major purchases. I don't recommend you use this kind of account for smaller purchases. Reserve this for emergencies, only.

You can also buy furniture the same way. A new sofa or bed mattresses need to be replaced about every 10 years or so, unless you have kids! When that time comes, there are many discount furniture stores that offer "same as cash accounts." Stay within your ability to pay. You will probably have 12 months to make your payments at no interest. To keep the cost down, look for discontinued items or "broken lots" with lowered prices.

Same as Cash accounts have actually been around for a long time. I remember buying my first vacuum cleaner this way. I picked it out, filled out some paperwork, and took it home. They gave me 6 months to pay if off – interest free. All of the appliances in my home and some of my furniture was financed over 12 months, 18 months or 24 months at a local home improvement or furniture retailer – all interest free. Payments of this kind fit nicely into a **Spending Plan**. It's a fixed amount and you aren't paying interest.

Chapter 7

Living in the Right Place

Apartment, Condo or House?

A lot was said about buying a home, which will prove to be your greatest investment. It's where most of your income will be applied. So, what if you can't buy a home right now?

You are not alone. For some, renting an apartment, condominium, town house, or house may be their best option. Military families often choose this option because they tend to get deployed. Perhaps you are between jobs or your credit needs improvement. Whatever the reason, renting a home can be the right thing to do.

There is a lot to consider when selecting rental property. You need to know if they take pets and how many. Sometimes they have a limit on the size of a pet. Then there is the deposit and the monthly "rent" for that pet.

If you have children, that's another thing to consider. Is there a playground on the premises and what is their policy concerning children?

Do they have laundry facilities or will you have to use a washeteria? Be sure to ask away, because what you don't know, can bother you later. Sometimes, we are so excited about getting our application approved, that we don't ask any questions. I, know, that was me.

I once rented a 1-bedroom apartment, only to find out that the W/D unit was an "apartment" sized unit and it simply did not handle all the clothes I washed every week. I had to do a load daily to keep up with it. Eventually, I found a washeteria nearby that did the job and I caught up on some reading!

The atmosphere or neighborhood where the rental property is located is also very important. After all, you are thinking about living there. Tour the complex in the daytime and then drive through there at night with your family or a friend. That can be a revelation. One place I saw looked great when the agent showed me around. When I drove through there at night, when residents returned home from work, I realized how limited the parking was and how narrow the streets were throughout the complex. It was a good place for fender benders for sure! Another place I toured in the daytime also looked great, but during my 11:00 PM cruise, I noticed a lot of wandering persons on the property with no place to go.

Another thing you can do is walk around the complex and speak to some of the residents – if you dare. They might share some information. Then again, what is pleasing to some may not be pleasing to others.

Check for signs of insect damage or insects. Water on

the premises of any kind, a fountain, lake or a pool attract these critters. If you decide this is the place for you anyway, get a unit away from the water and spray the premises on a regular basis.

One clue to a great apartment complex or rental community, is the grounds. Generally, if they keep the grounds up, they will come to replace your dish washer when it stops working.

Parking can be a challenge at some rental properties. Some places only allow you to park 1 vehicle. If you have 2, you may have to pay additional for an extra parking space. The visitor parking is sometimes limited as well. Find out where it is. Be sure your guests don't get towed!

Renting a House

Renting a home is very different from an apartment, condo or town house. A house requires you to maintain the yard and perhaps other things, which varies by property. For example, you will be responsible to mow the lawn, spray for insects and possibly provide your own appliances. The beauty of renting a home, though, is that it's a lot like owning your own home. At least, you can pretend!

Once you have lived in a rented house for a period of time, you will probably be thinking about home ownership. That is usually the next step. You will probably have a better idea of what you want in a house, after renting one. It will also help you decide if yardwork is for you and all the other do-it-yourself projects that incur with living in a house. Personally, I have lived in a two-family home (now town-house) a trailer, several apartments and a number of houses. Each has its own beauty and can meet the need, depending on your circumstance. The real deciding factor for renting a house, will be the amount of the rent! You will need to find something that fits your budget. And always, always, always, check that **Spending Plan** and see what you can afford.

As I have mentioned throughout this book, do your research. Ask around about apartments, condos, town homes and houses for rent and check online for the reviews. One last thought about renting an apartment, town house, condominium or house - READ THE CONTRACT.

Chapter 8
Car Buying

Autos etc.

So, you are ready to buy a car, truck or van. Start by looking at your **Spending Plan**. What can you afford without getting yourself in a situation? Are there any expenses you can trim down? Have you found any leaks in your spending that you need to tidy up? Once you have a figure, go to your own bank or credit union and find out how much car you can buy. It's done the same way as applying for a home loan. You will get pre-approved for a dollar amount and they will offer you the lowest interest rate. The dealership will not always give you the best interest rate. Then compare the monthly payment the bank gives you with your **Spending Plan**. They should come out to be about the same or close. The bank has the last word on what they will loan you, but if the bank figure it higher than your budgeted amount, go with the lower amount. The car is most likely a newer model so the insurance and property tax will increase. You want to have enough every month to cover this. Now that you know how much car you can afford, you are ready to look at cars.

There are several kinds of car dealerships. A regular car dealership will finance the car through a bank that they are affiliated with. It can be a higher interest rate than what you could get at your own bank. If you belong to a credit union, they offer car loans at a lower rate.

A "Buy Here, Pay Here" car lot offers you their financing and some advertise that you can get an approval in a matter of minutes. Compared to a regular dealership, a "Buy Here, Pay Here" dealer offers instant credit and rarely turns anyone down. It does have differing policies from a traditional dealership, so be aware of this before signing anything.

When you go to a regular dealership, just know there will be pressure. This is a good reason to know what you want. Research ahead of time the kind of vehicle you are interested in buying. Know everything you can about the make, model, features, etc. so you can sound like you know what you're talking about! Don't allow anyone to get over on you. And be prepared to spend a few hours at the dealership, negotiating the price. You can negotiate a lot: price, features, warranties, and free services like life-time oil changes and/or inspections. And get the extra key only one. However, I asked for the manager and insisted they make me another key, at their expense. Two weeks later, it was ready at the dealership for me to pick up. Do some of your own negotiating to get what you are looking for in a car. There is not harm in asking for a little help!

New or Used?

I have found that a slightly used car is the best deal. There are some reputable dealerships that deal only in used cars. They provide a document that lists everything about the car, truck or van and any history associated with it. They might be "fleet" cars that were previously rentals but the mileage is low and the price is considerably reduced. They are usually clean, and in good condition. Sometimes there are "demos" that were used by customers to test-drive a particular make or model. They are also in good or excellent condition and also have low mileage. I have purchased both types of vehicles and was very pleased. Then you can find used cars called, "Certified Pre-Owned" vehicles. You can go online and read up on this. These cars are warranted and provide the highest level of reliability for used cars, and it can save you a ton of money!

A used car is sold at considerable savings. A late-model used car that is only about 1-3 years old can sell for a lot less than a new car and give years of service. This would be my first choice if I was on a tight budget or trying to grow my savings account. For many, this is just being smart!

There is nothing like a brand-new car, though. Yes, it's the smell and the feel of new upholstery and all the features. I will tell you about a funny, but not-so-funny story, about my first, *special order* new car.

After doing my research about economy cars and a particular make and model, I decided on the sporty model, but with plenty of room. I won't mention the kind of car because this is not a sales promotion! I will tell you the color, though. It was magnesium metallic, with black interior, fully loaded. The day the dealership called to let me know that the car was there, I could hardly wait to see it. There it was, in the back lot, all wrapped in plastic. The salesperson pulled away the plastic around the door of the driver's side so I could sit inside. Wow! I just breathed in the fragrance. I was ready to take it home, when the salesman told me the car had to be detailed, first, and they had to "look it over." What? Why would you detail a new car?

I picked the car up a few days later and signed papers, etc. and drove it home. I parked the car in our driveway which is fenced on one side. The next day, my husband wanted to give me valet service so he backed the car out of the driveway, right into the fence. Oh my! You guessed it! There was a small dent and scraped paint along one side. I won't tell you the rest of that story, but then something else happened.

A few months later, my dear husband was mowing the yard and weed-eating the patio near the driveway. You guessed it again! A tiny rock flew up through the air and zapped out my taillight. It hit dead center! I believe I cried this time. But that's not all.

The following summer, I was driving home from work and stopped for a school bus near a railroad crossing. A person behind me, on a cell phone, did not see me or the bus (their own words) and crashed into the back of my magnesium metallic sporty car. Yes, that was the end of Maggie (my car). Complete total and 6 months at the chiropractor! Nothing against new cars, but something to think about. If it was a used car, I might not have been as upset. I did get very good insurance coverage from the responsible party and I was able to buy another new car. I even changed my insurance provider as a result. The offending party's company compensated me far more than my own insurance company would have!

To Trade or Not to Trade

If you have an old car and it is already paid for, that is the best trade. Look up the actual value of the vehicle beforehand, online. When negotiating a price, save this fact for the end. It's the ace in your hand. Stand firm and expect a reasonable offer from the dealership. You will probably have to name an exact price. Expect to get it, too. This amount will be subtracted from your total cost of your "new" car.

If you still owe on a car that is about 1 or 2 years old, and you want to trade it, they will offer to pay off your car and you start fresh with a new car payment. The problem here is that the money you paid on it, is essentially lost. It's like renting a very expensive car! In this case, ask for some compensation for those years. Here's where you could ask for a reduction in the cost of the new car you want to buy. The sales dept. has a lot of leverage in what they can give you on a trade-in or how they can work the deal. Don't be afraid to ask.

A car that is more than 3 years old with a note, is not a good trade. You probably owe more than the car is worth. This is what they refer to as, "upside down." You might try selling it outright or keep it for your teenager! Maybe you can fix it! You will lose if you try to trade. This is why knowing something about a car before you buy it is very important. You want to buy a car you will be happy with for a long time. If you finance the car for 5 years and it's paid off, then the next 5 -10 years after that, you won't have a car note. That's money you can put into your savings account.

Limit Car Notes

Do yourself a favor and avoid having two or more car notes at a time. Plan your purchases long-term so that you only pay for one vehicle for that 5 to 6-year span. It's perfectly ok to have one new car and one old car. It's just like the cell phone purchase. If you can't afford a *Superphone* then buy the flip phone. Buy the car that fits your budget knowing it's not going to put you into a financial crisis. It's a sad day when a car gets repossessed.

I remember the day a friend of mine was just getting off of work. He went to the parking lot to get in his car to drive home, and well, it was missing. He had no idea what happened to it and filed a police report. Turns out, he was behind on his payments for a couple of months and the dealership came and got it. Not only was he without transportation, but it ruined his credit for a long time. This is why you want to stay within your means and only buy what you can realistically afford.

Auto Purchase Checklist

1. Vehicle history report – disclosure
2. Overall performance on Test Drive
3. Mileage: after 60,000 will need major repairs
4. Signs of leaking fluids or corrosion on battery
5. The exterior/interior in good condition
6. A "lemon clause" in the contract
7. Mechanic's Assessment (get your own)

When you ask about the vehicle, expect full disclosure from the dealership or wherever you purchase the car or truck. Bring a mechanic friend if possible, who can help you with your own inspection.

And, before you actually buy a vehicle, be sure to test drive the car. Take it on the highway, as well as side streets. See how it handles during turns, when passing another vehicle and when stopping. While these may seem to be obvious, we can get so caught up in buying a car that we don't spend enough time checking the car out. Now, do what I've already mentioned for buying a home - go buy the book about buying cars. You will get more expert advice. This checklist is just a snapshot to get you on the road to success and check the tires!

Chapter 9

Loss Prevention

Insurance

Insurance of any kind is designed to cover the cost of loss. It could be for an auto accident, storm or flood damage, theft, medical care, and even death (Life insurance). Whatever insurance you purchase, be sure to find out exactly what it covers and the amount of the deductible and out of pocket expenses. Many of us tend to blindly trust the agent or the reputation of the provider and make a lot of assumptions. We fail to find out the details of our coverage. Also, consider the cost of premiums and how that fits into your spending plan.

One year, my area had extensive rain due to an offshore hurricane. The soaking rain caused water seepage under my house, which took days before I could get someone to extract the water from the crawl space. Unfortunately, this was not covered by my home owners insurance. It is *not* considered "water damage" but "flooding." Therefore, flood insurance was required to cover that cost. I was not living in a "flood zone" and was never alerted to this possibility when purchasing the home. So, you might want to get the flood insurance if your home is anywhere near the coast or near large bodies of water!

House Alarms

I wish I could tell you the name of the alarm company who holds my contract! Why I bought this thing, I'll never know. It goes off when it's not supposed to and doesn't work when it should. When you call the alarm service you get the run around.

One day my husband and I were taking a drive to a nearby city, about 40 minutes away from our home. It had been a long week for both of us and it was nice to get away for a few hours. Then we get the call. "Fire, fire." There was no fire. I called the alarm company and they confirmed that the smoke alarm needed new batteries. (They do this wirelessly, communicating with the panel box). So, they supposedly cancelled the call to the police, etc. but never did. The police were alerted, and the fire department and an ambulance showed up at the house. A neighbor sees them and calls us to tell us about it. We confirmed that there was no fire, that the smoke alarm needed batteries. So, the rescue team leaves. Then the smoke alarm goes off again and it starts over. Long story short, we had to drive back home. Forty minutes later, we were there and replaced the batteries. A few minutes later, it went off again so, we removed the offending smoke detector. I will spare you the details of my phone call to the alarm company. This was not the first time a day was interrupted or we had to make numerous phone calls or had parts replaced. I have also known friends and family who have had alarm systems installed and got robbed anyway. Then there's the neighbors' alarms that go off whenever the dog barks or the UPS driver drops something at the front door. What I have found to be effective is the right kind of locks, and it will cost you a whole lot less.

Lock it Up!

This is perhaps the wisest investment in loss prevention. There are all kinds of locks, not just padlocks or deadbolts, but, car locks, bike locks, and window locks, etc. My advice is to buy them and use them.

When you move into a new place, change all the locks. Buy the most expensive exterior locks you can afford. Make extra sets for lockouts and know where they are! Install deadbolts on every exterior door and in some cases replace the hinges or the whole door.

If your kids own a bike, buy them a lock. If you don't have a garage or shed, lock it to the railing or something stationary. If you live in an apartment, take it inside. Remind your kids to lock it up wherever they go as well. Here are a few other places to put locks and/or chains: gates, sheds, garage doors, storage buildings, lawn mowers (outside), ladders, gas grills (including the tank).

Inside the house, a good locking system is a file cabinet where you can store valuables such as files, personal information, legal documents (titles, deeds, birth certificates, etc.) sensitive information, or extra keys. I can't stress the need for a sturdy, 4-drawer, metal file cabinet that locks. A trespasser would have a hard time carrying this off.

Windows in a home also need metal locks. These are very inexpensive, and easy to install. For a price, you can also buy those metal bars that cover the entire window. This is a good option for children's windows or the back of the house.

They also make these metal exterior doors made of iron, that cover sliding glass doors. They are like French doors and they open outward. They can be locked from the inside. Sliding glass doors have been an easy access for stranger danger.

Depending on where you live or the type of home you have, decide what is best for your protection.

Now lest you think I'm paranoid, the use of locks is a standard procedure at every public place. Every bank, school, and retail store have a system of locks. Some businesses have huge metal gates that close at night. The local gym – think of all those lockers, the pawn shops, car dealerships and restaurants – they all use locks. In addition, there are security cameras in all the malls and many stores? They are there to protect you and STOP them.

Help, I Can't Find My Car!

Did you ever park your car somewhere and couldn't find it? If you're like a lot of people, it happened to you at least once! Yes, I know about the little red button on your car key, but sometimes that's not enough. It's easy to forget where you parked. "Losing" your car tends to happen because we are not mindful of where we parked it. We just park it, lock it and walk away. The problem arises when we come out of the airport terminal and have no idea where the car is and we have guests! Here are a few tips to help with this situation:

1. Write down the lot number (level #, row #, etc.) for the parking lot or the street name.
2. Remember any landmarks near your car such as a building, signs, statue or whatever.
3. Forget about remembering who was parked next to you. They may be gone when you get back!
4. If you are looking for your car, act like you know where it is.
5. If all else fails, call the police or security. They will need the make, model and tag # of your car. You do know your license plate number, right?

Gloves, Hats, Wind and Rain

By mid-winter, I often see one lost glove or hat in a parking lot, only to find the same thing in another place. Sometimes, it's a pair of gloves left behind in a restaurant or a hat in an elevator. How does this happen? I have a few suggestions for keeping up with this kind of stuff, too. Let's talk about gloves, first.

If you're in your car and just running into a store, just leave the gloves in the car. If you must wear them, then put them in your purse (women) or in an inside coat pocket (men) when you go inside the store. If you put them in the side pockets where you put your hands, they will probably fall out. Wherever you put them, it's a good idea to check periodically to see if they are still in place. And when you buy gloves, buy two pair!

Hats are tough because there's the wind factor. If it's a windy day, hold on to it or take it off and carry it. That's another item you see on the ground, especially during the winter. When you go to work with your hat, remove it once you get inside. Put it with your coat and other things, do the same with your gloves. The rest of the time, especially in public places, just wear your hat if at all possible.

My husband used to lose hats at restaurants. He would take it off (old school) and set it down and walk off without it.

We solved that problem by leaving it in the car. Sorry NY!

Then there are the umbrellas. I hesitate to say how many stadium umbrellas I have lost. However, once I started putting my name on them, they got returned more often. One way I would lose them is when I would go to someone's home or to church. Those nice people want to help you out and "check" your coat and umbrella! I found if I leave the umbrella in the car and make a mad dash to the building, that's better. If it's raining too hard, I carry it in and ask the hostess or usher to remind me of my umbrella before I leave. That has helped a lot.

While these little tips may or may not work for you, the real secret is to <u>become more aware</u> of what you are doing. We just don't pay attention to our stuff, sometimes. It's easy to get careless with our things and just leave it anywhere. Let's not talk about car keys!

Nowadays, I keep up with things a lot more. At bedtime, I have a spot where I put my glasses, which is on top of my tall dresser, next to the alarm clock. Previously, I misplaced them frequently. When I get up in the morning, I put the glasses on first and turn off the alarm. That has worked for me, for a long time now. I have done this for other things I used to hide from myself. You will come up with some ideas of your own. You just need a plan.

Where's My Receipt!

Remember that file cabinet I mentioned earlier? Well, you can also put your receipts in there. Go to one of those discount stores and buy a box of file folders. Choose 12 folders, preferably the ones where the tabs alternate from left, to right, to center. Label each folder individually with a month of the year. At the start of the year, put your receipts for the month of January in the folder, marked "January." You can also put paid bills in that same folder. File it in your file cabinet in one of the top 2 drawers. Continue to do this throughout the year. When you need to return something or verify a paid bill, there it is, all organized for you.

You can also keep track of all those owner's manuals that come with the microwave, refrigerator, lawn mower, etc. using that same file cabinet. Make file folders that include labels for each type of major purchase. You will find this to be useful when trying to retrieve information about yard tools or appliances. You can also keep the original receipt for that purchase with the manual. I also write the date of purchase on the manual itself. *See Chart on page 74.*

I cannot tell you how helpful this will be. For years, we just put manuals anywhere. When a power tool or mower needed a part, we had no idea where the book was. Last year, the mower we were using needed to be replaced. When I found the manual, in the file cabinet, I discovered it lasted 12 years. The date was written on the manual! This assured me it was time for a new one. *Not* having this information can cost you.

One year I needed 2 new tires. I took the car to the dealership where I got most of my maintenance done and bought 2 new tires. The tires were installed, balanced and rotated. I also had an alignment. When I got home and pulled out my **Auto Maintenance** file, I discovered that my old tires were still under warranty (I bought them at a tire store). Wow! So, obviously I paid for something I didn't need to pay for. So, be sure to check your files before paying for repairs or replacements. It just might be under warranty!

Car inspections are sometimes free at the dealership where you bought the car. The same is true for oil changes. When you buy a new car, lifetime oil changes or something similar is part of the contract. Again, check the contract under **Legal Documents** before paying for anything.

On the next page, you will find a suggested list of possible file folders for storing your owner's manuals, warranties, legal documents and the like. It can be a real life saver!

*Examples of **File folders** to help you get things organized:*

FILE FOLDERS FOR OWNER'S MANUALS
Auto Maintenance (oil changes, tires, repairs)
Furniture (beds, tables, chairs, sofas, etc.)
Home Warranty
HVAC (Furnace, A/C, water heater)
Large Appliances (range, refrigerator, dish washer, etc.)
Lawn & Garden (grill, furniture, planters, etc.)
Plumbing
Power Tools (drill, circular saw, grinder, sander)
Legal Documents (contracts, certificates, auto titles, etc.)
Small Appliances (microwave, mixer, food processor)
Sports Equipment (bicycles, helmets, weights, etc.)
Windows & Doors (interior and exterior)
Uniforms, Safety Equipment
Yard Equipment (lawn mower, blower, weed-eater)

Chapter 10

Live Right

Your Dreams

Everyone has had a dream sometime in their life. They may be short-term or long-term goals. Whatever you aspire to do, remember that you must have a plan. If you have made it this far in my book, then you have read the word "plan" perhaps 50 times. That's the real message of this book. Develop a **Spending Plan** that helps you live the life you have always dreamed of. If you are just going about your daily life on auto-pilot or just haphazardly doing things, this is counterproductive. Whether it's buying the right home or car, keeping up with your hat and gloves or avoiding wasteful spending, all of these things contribute to right living.

My hope is that you will take the time to review the ideas presented in this book and follow a plan that maximizes your spending and living capacity. And remember to **Spend Right and Live Right!**

"It takes as much energy to wish as it does to plan."
-Eleanor Roosevelt

*I have included a blank **Spending Plan** for you to practice:*

TAKE HOME PAY - Monthly	
TOTAL	

*Here are examples of the **Envelope system** for CASH, only.*

Gasoline	Food
Haircut	Pet supplies
Weekends	School
Birthdays	Music Lessons
Babysitter	Misc.

[This page intentionally left blank]